Planes have been around for quite a long time.

Modern planes look a bit different from early planes, but they all have wings and a cockpit.

older plane

modern plane

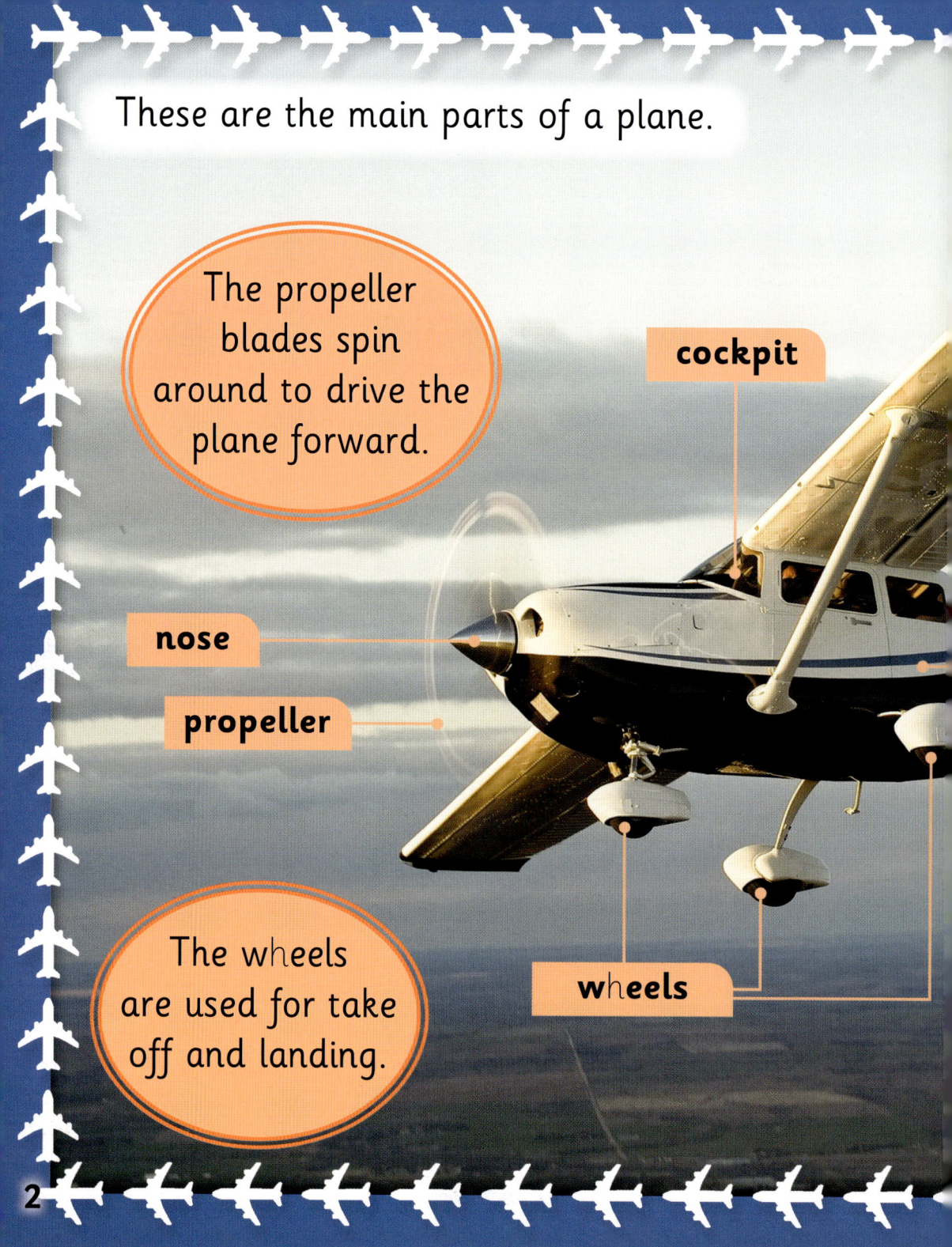

These are the main parts of a plane.

The propeller blades spin around to drive the plane forward.

cockpit

nose

propeller

The wheels are used for take off and landing.

wheels

The wings lift the plane.

The tail helps to keep the plane steady as it flies.

rudder

wing

tail

body

The cockpit is where the pilot (/**pie**lɛt/) sits.

The wings have some important smaller parts.

The winglets at the ends of a plane's wings help the plane to travel more smoothly.

The slats, flaps, ailerons and spoilers are used to steer the plane and control its speed as it takes off, flies and lands.

Not all planes have a propeller. Bigger planes and jets have jet engines (/**en**jinz/) under the wings instead. These thrust the plane forward, just like propellers do.

jet engines

This is a close up. You can see the propeller-like fan blades inside.

There are lots of different sorts of planes.

There are small planes, which can be for just one person...

...there are big planes, which can carry hundreds...

...and there are cargo planes, which only carry objects.

This small plane is called a glider (or sometimes a sailplane). A glider normally has no engine (/**en**jin/). Instead, it has a thin body and very wide wings, which help it to soar and glide.

long, thin wings

glider

long, thin body

Early gliders were made from heavy things, such as wood, metal and canvas, but modern gliders are made to be strong without being heavy.

This small plane has two sets of wings. It is called a biplane (/**bie**plain/).

Early planes often had two sets of wings.

This plane was invented and built in 1903 by the Wright brothers (riet **bru**therz).

Sometimes, biplanes are used for tricks and stunts. One such stunt involves a person standing on the wings of a plane as it flies!

This man is doing tricks and flips as the plane flies. He is attached to the plane, but it is still a risky thing to do.

Small jets can be used to do tricks and stunts, as well.

These jets are doing a loop-the-loop.

These jets are going straight up, which is a very difficult thing to do in a plane.

Big passenger (/**pa**ssenjer/) planes are very common. They carry travellers from country to country, or across a big country.

The passengers go up the steps to board (get on) the plane.

Then they sit inside the cabin.

This is what the inside of a passenger plane looks like.

Plane travel is quick and quite common, but it is not good for the planet. Planes use fossil fuels, which harm the planet.

This plane is called Concorde. It was a sort of passenger plane.

Concorde was a French and British plane. It had a characteristic drooping nose.

drooping nose

Concorde was very speedy indeed. In fact, it travelled more quickly than sound itself!

When a plane goes more quickly than the speed of sound, there is a sonic boom (a very loud bang noise).

Concorde was very expensive to run and extremely noisy, so we no longer use it.

Cargo planes are used to transport very big things across the planet.

A cargo plane has a very long, wide body so that it can carry big objects.

This is what a cargo plane looks like inside.

Did you know that a plane can trigger a thunderstorm when it flies in a cloud?

This sounds alarming, but you do not need to worry. It is very unlikely that lightning will harm the plane.